AN EASY GUIDE TO THE HAWAIIAN LANGUAGE

Jade Mapuana Riley

MUTUAL PUBLISHING

Dedicated to my four children—
Kalahulani, Kekainani, Mikaʻele, and
Maluhia Riley.

ISBN-10: 1-56647-715-8
ISBN-13: 978-1-56647-715-4

Library of Congress Catalog Card Number: 2005920875

First Printing, May 2005
Second Printing, April 2007
Third Printing, February 2008
Fourth Printing, April 2009
Fifth Printing, April 2010
Sixth Printing, January 2011
Seventh Printing, September 2011
Eighth Printing, April 2012
Ninth Printing, May 2013
Tenth Printing, April 2014
Eleventh Printing, June 2015
Twelfth Printing, June 2016
Thirteenth Printing, June 2017

Mutual Publishing, LLC
1215 Center Street, Suite 210
Honolulu, Hawaiʻi 96816
Ph: 808-732-1709 / Fax: 808-734-4094
email: info@mutualpublishing.com
www.mutualpublishing.com
Printed in Taiwan

Table of Contents

Introduction

Aloha! As a student years ago studying Hawaiian, I found myself searching for an easy guide, a simple introduction to the Hawaiian language. Basic, common, overall useful daily tips. I believe this is really how the idea of this guide came about.

This is an easy reference guide to numerous Hawaiian words.

Many Hawaiian words have multiple meanings. This handy household guide offers the most common definitions, a simplified pronunciation guide, and the most common usage of each word in everyday conversations. Use the pronunciation guide as it is written. There is no need to analyze or overemphasize.

It is written in English-Hawaiian translation, and by categories for quick referencing. Both parents and children will find this guide very helpful as it introduces them to numerous Hawaiian words, as well as being a basic introduction to the Hawaiian language.

For more detailed information on the Hawaiian language, I suggest Mary Kawena Pukui's Hawaiian-English dictionary.

The Alphabets (nā pi'apa)

The Hawaiian alphabet consists of thirteen letters: five vowels and eight consonants.

> Vowels: a, e, i, o, u
> Consonants: h, k, l, m, n, p, w, and the okina(')

The vowels have two sounds, stressed and unstressed. Vowels with a bar, called the KAHAKO (ā) in Hawaiian, are pronounced by drawing out the sound and are always stressed.

The Hawaiian language is full of glottal stops, called the 'OKINA ('). Those have a very slight pause, as occurs between "oh-oh."

HELPFUL PRONUNCIATION TIPS
FOR THIS GUIDE:

The pronunciation guide for this book was written in the simplest form for easy guidance in pronouncing each word. There is no need to overemphasize. Take your time, pronounce it slowly, repeat and have fun.

a, as in water	**ā**, as in ah
e, as in wet	**ē**, as in hey
i, as in bit	**ī**, as in police
o, as in obey	**ō**, as in bow
u, as in pull	**ū**, as in spoon

Two vowel combinations usually merge as a *diphthong*, some examples beings:

ou, as in soul	**ai**, like "i" in light
oi, as in loiter	**au**, like "ou" in out
ae, like "y" in my	**ao**, like "ow" in how
ei, as in veil	

WHEN PLURALIZING:

There is no "s" in the Hawaiian Language. One easy and basic way to pluralize a word in Hawaiian is to simply put "NĀ" before the word.

Examples:

Book	*puke* (poo-kay)
Books	*nā puke*
Eye	*maka* (ma-kah)
Eyes	*nā maka*

Greetings & Everyday Short Phrases

Hello/Goodbye/ Greetings
aloha
(ah-low-hah)

Good morning
aloha kakahiaka
(ah-low-hah kah-kah-he-ah-kah)

Good afternoon (midday)
aloha awakea
(ah-low-hah ah-vah-kay-ah)

Good afternoon
aloha ʻauinalā
(ah-low-hah ow-we-nah-lah)

Good evening (night)
aloha ahiahi
(ah-low-hah ah-he-ah-he)

Thank you
mahalo
(ma-hah-low)

Thank you very much
mahalo a nui loa
(ma-hah-low ah noo-ee low-ah)

Please
ke ʻoluʻolu
(kay oh-lou-oh-lou)

You're welcome (No problem)
ʻaʻole pilikia
(ah-oh-lay pee-lee-key-ah)

Yes	*'ae* (eye)
No	*'a'ole* (ah-oh-lay)
Excuse me **(I'm sorry)** .	*e kala mai ia'u* (eh kah-lah my-ee yah-oo)
How are you	*pehea 'oe* (pay-hay-yah oy)
Fine/Good	*maika'i* (my-kah-ee)
Come in	*e komo mai* (eh koh-moh my)
See you later	*a hui hou* (ah who-ee ho)
Take care	*mālama pono* (ma-lah-ma poh-no)
Do it again/Encore	*hana hou* (hah-nah ho)
What (who) **is your name**	*'O wai kou inoa* (oh vye koh ee-no-ah)

My name is (…)	*'O (…) ko'u inoa* (oh (…) koh-oo ee-no-ah)
Okay	*hiki nō* (he-key no)
Very good	*maika'i loa* (my-kah-ee low-ah)
I don't know (It is not clear to me)	*'a'ole maopopo ia'u* (ah-oh-lay mow-poh-poh yah-oo)
Is the best	*nō ka 'oi* (no-ka-oy)

Helpful Everyday Words

A	*he/kekahi* (hay)/(kay-kah-he)
At, in, on	*ma/i* (ma)/(ee)
Because	*no/no ka mea* (no-kah-may-ah)
But	*akā* (ah-kah)
He, she, it	*ia* (yah)
His, hers	*kona* (koh-nah)
I	*au/wau* (ow)/(vow)
My	*koʻu* (koh-oo)
Now (At this time)	*i kēia manawa* (ee kay-ee-ah ma-nah-vah)

Sometime/ Sometimes	*kekahi manawa* (kay-kah-he ma-nah-vah)	
That	*kēlā* (kay-lah)	
The	*ka/ke* (kah)/(kay)	
This	*kēia* (kay-ee-ah)	
To	*i* (ee)	
What?	*he aha* (hay ah-hah)	
Where?	*i hea* (ee hay-ah)	
Who?	*wai* (vye)/(why)	
With	*me* (may)	
You (one person)	*'oe* (oy)	
Your	*kou* (koh)	

Basic Helpful Commands

Come with me	E hele mai 'oe me a'u (eh hey-lay my oy may yah-oo)
Sit down	*E noho i lalo* (eh no-ho ee lah-low)
Be careful	*E akahele* (eh ah-kah-hey-lay)
Stand up	*E kū i luna* (eh koo ee lou-nah)
Shut the door	*E pani i ka puka* (eh pah-nee ee kah poo-kah)
Listen	*E ho'olohe mai* (eh ho-oh-low-hey my)
Give it to me	*E hā'awi mai ia'u* (eh hah-ah-vee my yah-oo)
Get your slippers	*E ki'i 'oe i kou mau kalipa* (eh key-ee oy ee koh mow kah-lee-pah)
Wash your hands	*E hōloi i kou lima* (eh ho-loy ee koh lee-ma)

Brush your teeth	*E palaki i kou niho*	
	(eh pah-lah-key ee koh nee-ho)	
Let's sing	*E hīmeni kākou*	
	(eh he-many kah-koh)	
Let's pray	*E pule kākou*	
	(eh poo-lay kah-koh)	
Let's eat	*E 'ai kākou*	
	(eh eye kah-koh)	
Let's go	*E hele kākou*	
	(eh hey-lay kah-koh)	
Come inside	*E komo i loko*	
	(eh koh-moh ee low-koh)	
Throw away the rubbish	*E kiloi i na 'ōpala*	
	(eh key-loy ee nah oh-pah-lah)	
Close your eyes	*Pani i kou mau maka*	
	(pah-nee ee koh mow ma-kah)	
Don't do that	*Mai hana pēlā*	
	(my hah-nah pay-lah)	
Don't run; walk quietly	*Mai holo; e hele mālie*	
	(my ho-low, eh hey-lay ma-lee-eh)	

Verbs/Action Words

To come	*hele mai* (hay-lay my)
To go	*hele aku* (hay-lay ah-koo)
To run/sail	*holo* (ho-low)
To walk/ride	*holoholo* (ho-low-ho-low)
To listen for pleasure	*hoʻolohe* (ho-oh-low-hay)
To sing	*hīmeni* (he-may-nee)
To prepare, make ready	*hoʻomākaukau* (ho-oh-ma-cow-cow)
To call	*kāhea* (kah-hay-ah)
To stand, stop	*kū* (koo)
To jump, fly	*lele* (lay-lay)
To look	*nānā* (nah-nah)
To sit	*noho* (no-ho)

More Short Phrases You Can Use

I'm tired

māluhiluhi wau
(ma-lou-he-lou-he vow)

I'm sick

ma'i wau
(ma-ee vow)

What is this?

he aha kēia
(hey ah-hah kay-ee-ah)

What is that?

he aha kēlā
(hey ah-hah kay-lah)

What did you do?
(What are you
going to do?)

he aha kāu hana
(hey ah-hah cow hah-nah)

Where are you?

ai hea 'oe
(eye hay-yah oy)

Where are you going?
(You are going where)

e hele ana 'oe i hea
(eh hey-lay ah-nah
oy ee hay-ah)

Where is your slipper?

māhea kou kalipa
(ma-hey-ah koh
kah-lee-pah)

Do you understand?   *ua maopopo iā'oe*
(mow-poh-poh yah oy)

Be quiet   *e pa'a i kou waha*
(eh pah-ah ee
koh wah-hah)

Who is that?   *'o wai kēlā*
(oh vye kay-lah)

How is the teacher?   *pehea ke kumu*
(pay-hey-yah
kay koo-moo)

Family ('ohana)

Father	*makua kāne* (ma-koo-ah kah-nay)
Mother	*makuahine* (ma-koo-ah-he-nay)
Child	*keiki/kama* (kay-key) / (kah-ma)
Grandfather/ Grandmother	*kupuna kāne/kupuna wahine* (koo-poo-nah kah-nay)/ (koo-poo-nah wah-he-nay)
Son	*keiki kāne* (kay-key kah-nay)
Daughter	*kaikamahine* (ky-kah-ma-he-nay)
Uncle	*'anakala* (ah-nah-kah-lah)
Aunty	*'anakē* (ah-nah-kay)
Grandchild	*mo'opuna* (mo-oh-poo-nah)
Baby	*pēpē* (peh-peh)

Parts of the Body (kino)

Head	*po'o* (poh-oh)
Hair	*lauoho* (lau-oh-ho)
Eye	*maka* (ma-kah)
Ear	*pepeiao* (pay-pay-ya-ow)
Nose	*ihu* (ee-who)
Cheek	*papālina* (pah-pah-lee-nah)
Mouth	*waha* (wah-hah)
Shoulder	*po'ohiwi* (poh-oh-he-vee)
Bosom	*poli* (poh-lee)

Hand/Arm	*lima*	
	(lee-ma)	
Stomach	*'ōpū*	
	(oh-poo)	
Foot/Leg	*wāwae*	
	(vah-vye)	
Knee	*kuli*	
	(koo-lee)	
Tooth	*niho*	
	(nee-ho)	
Eyelashes	*lihilihi*	
	(lee-he-lee-he)	
Eyebrow	*ku'emaka*	
	(koo-eh-ma-kah)	
Finger	*manamana lima*	
	(ma-nah-ma-nah lee-ma)	
Toe	*manamana wāwae*	
	(ma-nah-ma-nah vah-vye)	

Days of the Week

Monday   *Pō‘akahi*
                (poh-ah-kah-he)

Tuesday   *Pō‘alua*
                (poh-ah-lou-ah)

Wednesday   *Pō‘akolu*
                (poh-ah-koh-lou)

Thursday   *Pō‘ahā*
                (poh-ah-hah)

Friday   *Pō‘alima*
                (poh-ah-lee-ma)

Saturday   *Pō‘aono*
                (poh-ah-oh-no)

Sunday   *Lāpule*
                (lah-poo-lay)

Months of the Year

January	*'Ianuali* (yah-new-ah-lee)
February	*Pepeluali* (peh-peh-lou-ah-lee)
March	*Malaki* (ma-lah-key)
April	*'Apelila* (ah-pay-lee-lah)
May	*Mei* (may-ee)
June	*Iune* (you-nay)
July	*Iulai* (you-lye)
August	*'Aukake* (ow-kah-kay)
September	*Kepakemapa* (kay-pah-kay-ma-pah)
October	*'Okakopa* (oh-kah-koh-pah)
November	*Nowemapa* (no-way-ma-pah)/(no-veh-ma-pah)
December	*Kēkēmapa* (kay-kay-ma-pah)
Calendar	*'alemanaka* (ah-lay-ma-nah-kah)
Today	*i kēia lā* (ee kay-ee-ah lah)

Tomorrow	*i ka lā ʻāpōpō* (ee kah lah ah-poh-poh)
Yesterday	*i nehinei* (ee nay-he-nay-ee)
Last night	*i ka pō nei* (ee kah poh nay)
Tonight	*i kēia pō* (ee kay-ee-yah poh)
Week	*pule* (poo-lay)
Month	*mahina* (ma-he-nah)
Year	*makahiki* (ma-kah-he-key)

Time (ka manawa)

Start	*ho'omaka* (ho-oh-ma-kah)
Finish	*pau*/(pow)
On time	*i ka hola kūpono* (ee kah ho-lah koo-poh-no)
Late	*lohi* (low-he)
Minute	*mīnuke* (me-noo-kay)
Hour	*hola* (ho-lah)

Holidays (nā lanui)

Happy New Year   *Hauʻoli Makahiki Hou*
                          (how-oh-lee
                          ma-kah-he-key hoh)

Happy Birthday   *Hauʻoli Lā Hānau*
                          (how-oh-lee lah hah-now-oo)

Happy Anniversary   *Hauʻoli Piha Makahiki*
                          (how-oh-lee pee-hah
                          ma-kah-he-key)

Happy Thanksgiving   *Hauʻoli Lā Hoʻomaikaʻi*
                          (how-oh-lee lah
                          ho-oh-my-kah-ee)

Merry Christmas   *Mele Kalikimaka*
                          (may-lay
                          kah-lee-key-ma-kah)

Weather

Cloudy	*'ōmalumalu* (oh-ma-lou-ma-lou)
Hot	*wela* (veh-lah)
Wet	*pulu* (poo-lou)
Dry	*malo'o* (ma-low-oh)
Humid	*ikiiki* (ee-keee-key)
Warm	*mehana* (may-hah-nah)
Cool (chilly)	*hu'ihu'i* (who-ee-who-ee)
Cold	*anu/anuanu* (ah-noo-ah-noo)
Mist	*'ohu* (oh-who)

Rain	*ua*
	(oo-ah)
Wind	*makani*
	(mā-kah-nee)
Calm	*mālie*
	(ma-lee-eh)
Storm	*'ino*
	(ee-no)
Thunder	*hekili*
	(hey-key-lee)
Lightning	*uila/uwila*
	(oo-we-lah)
Rainbow	*ānuenue*
	(ah-noo-eh-noo-eh)
Pleasant	*'olu'olu*
	(oh-lou-oh-lou)

Direction ('okuhi)

Toward the sea   *makai*
(ma-ky)

Toward the mountain *mauka*
(mow-kah)

Up   *i luna*
(ee lou-nah)

Down   *i lalo*
(ee lah-low)

Forward   *i mua*
(ee moo-ah)

Backward   *i hope*
(ee ho-pay)

Here   *ma'ane'i*
(ma-ah-nay-ee)

There   *ma'ō*
(ma-oh)

Open   *hāmama/wehe*
(hah-ma-ma)/(vay-hey)

Close	*pani*	(pah-nee)
Near	*kokoke*	(koh-koh-kay)
Far	*mamao*	(ma-mow)
Inside	*i loko*	(ee-low-koh)
Outside	*i waho*	(ee-vah-ho)
Turn left	*e huli hema*	(eh who-lee hey-ma)
Turn right	*e huli ʻākau*	(eh who-lee ah-cow)
Go straight	*e hele pololei*	(eh hey-lay poh-low-lay)

Colors (nā waiho'olu'u)

Red	*'ula'ula*	(oo-lah-oo-lah)
Green	*'ōma'oma'o*	(oh-ma-oh-ma-oh)
Orange	*'alani*	(ah-lah-nee)
Purple	*poni*	(poh-nee)
Blue	*polū/uliuli*	(poh-lou)/(oo-lee-oo-lee)
Black	*'ele'ele*	(eh-lay-eh-lay)
Pink	*'ākala*	(ah-kah-lah)
White	*ke'oke'o*	(kay-oh-kay-oh)
Gold	*kula*	(koo-lah)
Silver/Gray	*'āhinahina*	(ah-he-nah-he-nah)
Brown	*māku'e*	(ma-koo-eh)
Yellow	*melemele*	(may-lay-may-lay)

Numbers (nā helu)

One	*'ekahi*	
	(eh-kah-he)	
Two	*'elua*	
	(eh-lou-ah)	
Three	*'ekolu*	
	(eh-koh-lou)	
Four	*'ehā*	
	(eh-ha)	
Five	*'elima*	
	(eh-lee-ma)	
Six	*'eono*	
	(eh-oh-no)	
Seven	*'ehiku*	
	(eh-he-koo)	
Eight	*'ewalu*	
	(eh-vah-lou)	
Nine	*'eiwa*	
	(eh-ee-vah)	

Ten	*'umi* (oo-me)
Eleven	*'umi kūmākahi* (oo-me-koo-ma-kah-he)
Twelve	*'umi kūmālua* (oo-me-koo-ma-lou-ah)

The numbers continue on through 19, in the same manner. Combining number (10/'umi), then the word (kūmā), then dropping the ('e) from numbers (1 through 9) and adding the last part of each number after the word (kūmā).

Another Example (#13):
'umi-10 + kūmā, drop ('e in 'ekolu, which is #3) = 'umi kūmākolu—#13.

Twenty	*iwakālua* (ee-vah-kah-lou-ah)
Twenty-one	*iwakālua kūmākahi* (ee-vah-kah-lou-ah koo-ma-kah-he)
Twenty-two	*iwakālua kūmālua* (ee-vah-kah-lou-ah koo-ma-lou-ah)

Continue on through number (29), using same pattern.

Thirty	*kanakolu* (kah-nah-koh-lou)
Forty	*kanahā* (kah-nah-hah)
Fifty	*kanalima* (kah-nah-lee-ma)
Sixty	*kanaono* (kah-nah-oh-no)
Seventy	*kanahiku* (kah-nah-he-koo)
Eighty	*kanawalu* (kah-nah-vah-lou)
Ninety	*kanaiwa* (kah-nah-ee-vah)
Ninety-one	*kanaiwa kūmākahi* (kah-nah-ee-vah koo-ma-kah-he)
Ninety-nine	*kanaiwa kūmāiwa* (kah-nah-ee-vah koo-ma-ee-vah)

One hundred	*ho'okahi haneli*	
	(ho-oh-kah-he hah-nel-ee)	
Two hundred	*'elua haneli*	
	(eh-lou-ah hah-nel-ee)	
Five hundred	*'elima haneli*	
	(eh-lee-ma hah-nel-ee)	
One thousand	*ho'okahi kaukani*	
	(ho-oh-kah-he cow-kah-nee)	

Animals (nā holoholona)

Bird	*manu* (ma-noo)
Cat	*pōpoki* (poh-poh-key)
Cattle/Cow	*pipi* (pee-pee)
Chicken	*moa* (mo-ah)
Dog	*'īlio* (ee-lee-oh)
Goat	*kao* (cow)
Hawaiian hawk	*'io* (ee-oh)
Horse	*lio* (lee-oh)
Lizard	*mo'o* (moh-oh)
Monkey	*keko* (kay-koh)
Mule	*hoki* (ho-key)
Owl	*pueo* (poo-eh-oh)
Pig	*pua'a* (poo-ah-ah)
Rabbit	*lāpaki* (lah-pah-key)
Rat	*'iole* (ee-oh-lay)

In the House (i loko i ka hale)

House	*hale* (hah-lay)
Room	*lumi* (lou-me)

Kitchen (lumi kuke):

Water	*wai* (vye)
Food	*mea ʻai* (may-yah eye)
Cup	*kīʻaha* (key-ah-hah)
Plate	*pā* (pah)
Spoon	*puna* (poo-nah)
Fork	*ʻō* (oh)
Knife	*pahi* (pah-he)
Napkin	*kāwele* (kah-veh-lay)

Cooking pot	*ipu hao* (ee-poo how)
Refrigerator	*pahu hau* (pah-who how)
Sponge	*'ūpī* (oo-pee)

Living Room (lumi ho'okipa):

Television (T.V.)	*kīwī* (kee-vee)
Door **(Hole through something)**	*puka* (poo-kah)
Couch **(movable couch)**	*pūne'e* (poo-nay-eh)
Couch **(large couch)**	*hikie'e* (he-key-eh-eh)
Rocking chair	*noho paipai* (no-ho pie-pie)
Telephone	*kelepona* (kay-lay-poh-nah)

Dining Room (lumi 'aina):

Dining table	*papa 'aina* (pah-pah eye-nah)

Chair	*noho* (no-ho)
Window	*pukaaniani* (poo-kah-ah-nee-ah-nee)
Light (electric)	*kukui uila* (koo-koo-ee oo-ee-lah)
Dinner Party/ Party	*pā'ina* (pah-ee-nah)
Meal	*aha'aina* (ah-hah-eye-nah)

Bathroom (lumi 'au'au):

Bath	*'au'au* (ow-ow)
Soap	*kopa* (koh-pah)
Bath towel	*kāwele 'au'au* (kah-veh-lay ow-ow)
Toilet	*lua* (lou-ah)
Toilet paper	*pepa hāleu* (pay-pah hah-lay-oo)
Bathtub	*kapu 'au'au* (kah-poo ow-ow)

| Toothbrush | *palaki niho* (pah-lah-key nee-ho) |
| Hairbrush | *palaki lauoho* (pah-lah-key lau-oh-ho) |

Bedroom (lumi moe):

To sleep	*hiamoe* (he-ah-moy)
Bed	*moena* (moy-nah)
Blanket	*kapa moe* (kah-pah moy)
Pillow	*uluna* (oo-lou-nah)
Closet	*waihona* (why-ho-nah)/(vye-ho-nah)
Dresser	*pahu waihona* (pah-who why-ho-nah)
Shelf	*haka* (hah-kah)
Bedsheet/Spread	*hāli'i moe* (hah-lee-ee moy)

Clothing (nā lole):

| Dress (garment) | *lole* (low-lay) |
| Slipper | *kalipa/pale wāwae* (kah-lee-pah)/(pah-lay vah vye) |

Shoe	*kāmaʻa*	(kah-ma-ah)
Shirt	*pālule*	(pah-lou-lay)
Undershirt	*paleʻili*	(pah-lay-ee-lee)
Pants	*lole wāwae*	(low-lay vah-vye)
Underwear	*palemaʻi/paleʻaʻahu*	(pah-lay-ma-ee)/ (pah-lay-ah-ah-who)
Hat	*pāpale*	(pah-pah-lay)
Jacket	*lakeke*	(lah-kay-kay)

Outside the House (i waho i ka hale)

Car	*ka'a* (kah-ah)
Truck	*kalaka* (kah-lah-kah)
Yard (fence/wall)	*pā* (pah)
Plant (crops)	*mea kanu* (may-yah kah-noo)
Tree	*kumulā'au* (koo-moo-lah-ow)
Seed	*'ano'ano* (ah-no-ah-no)
Flower	*pua* (poo-ah)
Ti leaf	*lā'ī* (lah-ee)
Coconut tree trunk	*kumu niu* (koo-moo nee-oo)
Fern	*kupukupu* (koo-poo-koo-poo)
Grass	*mau'u* (mow-oo)
Dirt/Soil	*lepo* (lay-po)
Shade	*malu* (ma-lou)
Thorn	*kukū* (koo-kooo)
Bucket	*pākeke* (pah-kay-kay)

Shovel	*kopalā*	(koh-pah-laa)
Rake	*kope*	(koh-pay)
Street	*alanui*	(ah-lah-noo-ee)
Town	*kaona*	(cow-nah)
Store	*hale kū'ai*	(hah-lay koo-eye)
Fire	*ahi*	(ah-he)
Island	*mokupuni*	(moh-koo-poo-nee)
Mountain	*mauna*	(mow-nah)
Cliff	*pali*	(pah-lee)
Pond	*loko wai*	(low-koh-vye)
Land	*'āina*	(eye-nah)
Sun	*lā*	(lah)
Cloud	*ao*	(ow)
Star	*hōkū*	(ho-koo)
Moon	*mahina*	(ma-he-nah)

Flowers & Fruits (nā pua & nā hua 'ai)

Carnation	*ponimō'ī* (poh-nee-moh-ee)
Ginger	*'awapuhi* (ah-vah-poo-he)
Hibiscus	*aloalo* (ah-low-ah-low)
Orchid	*'okika* (oh-key-kah)
Plumeria	*melia* (may-lee-ah)
Rose	*loke* (low-kay)
Banana	*mai'a* (my-ah)
Breadfruit	*'ulu* (oo-lou)
Coconut	*niu* (nee-oo)
Guava	*kuawa* (koo-ah-vah)
Mango	*manakō* (ma-na-koh)
Papaya	*mīkana* (me-kah-nah)
Passion fruit	*liliko'i* (lee-lee-koh-ee)

The Beach (kahakai)

Sea	*kai* (ky)
Ocean	*moana* (moh-ah-nah)
Sand	*one* (oh-nay)
Shell	*pūpū* (poo-poo)
Fish	*i'a* (ee-ah)
Shark	*manō* (ma-no)
Whale (humpback)	*koholā* (koh-ho-lah)
Turtle	*honu* (ho-noo)
Crab	*pāpa'i* (pah-pah-ee)
Eel	*puhi* (poo-he)

Lobster	*ula* (oo-lah)
Porpoise	*nai'a* (nye-ah)
Seaweed	*limu* (lee-moo)
Rock/Stone	*pōhaku* (poh-hah-koo)
Bay	*hono-/hana-* (ho-no)/(hah-nah)
Harbor	*awa* (ah-vah)
Surf/Wave	*nalu* (nah-lou)
Surfboard	*papa he'e nalu* (pah-pah hay-eh nah-lou)
Manta ray	*hāhālua* (hah-hah-lou-ah)
Portuguese man-o-war	*po'imalau* (poh-ee-ma-lau-oo)

At Work (ma hana)

To work	*hana* (hah-nah)
Boss	*luna* (lou-nah)
Customer	*mea kū'ai mai* (may-ah koo-eye my)
Office	*ke'ena* (kay-eh-nah)
Key	*kī* (key)
Bag/Purse	*'eke* (eh-kay)
Eyeglasses	*makaaniani* (ma-kah-ah-nee-ah-nee)
Watch/Clock	*uaki/uwaki* (oo-ah-key/oo-wah-key)
Money	*kālā* (kah-lah)
Table	*pākaukau* (pah-cow-cow)

At School (hale kula)

Schoolteacher	*kumu kula* (koo-moo-koo-lah)
Student	*haumāna* (how-ma-nah)
Friend	*hoaloha* (ho-ah-low-hah)
Classmate	*hoa kula* (ho-ah koo-lah)
Bus	*ka'a 'ōhua* (kah-ah oh-who-ah)
Paper	*pepa* (pay-pah)
Pen	*peni* (pay-nee)
Pencil	*penikala* (pay-nee-kah-lah)

Class	*papa*	(pah-pah)
Book	*puke*	(poo-kay)
Blackboard	*papa 'ele'ele*	(pah-pah-eh-lay-eh-lay)
Chalk	*poho*	(poh-ho)
Scissors	*'ūpā*	(oo-pah)
Marker	*māka*	(maa-kah)
Games/Toys	*mea pā'ani*	(may-ah pah-ah-nee)
Slide	*pahe'e*	(pah-hay-eh)
Glue	*kolū*	(koh-lou)

Toys (nā mea paʻani)

Ball/Baseball	*kinipōpō* (key-nee-poh-poh)
Balloon	*pāluna* (pah-lou-nah)
Basketball	*kinipōpō hīnaʻi* (key-nee-poh-poh he-nah-ee)
Bat (for ball)	*lāʻau kinipōpō* (lah-ow key-nee-poh-poh)
Bicycle	*paikikala* (pie-key-kah-lah)
Doll	*kiʻi pēpē* (key-ee pay-pay)
Football	*kinipōpō peku* (key-nee-poh-poh pay-koo)
Kite	*lupe* (lou-pay)
Marbles	*kinikini* (key-nee-key-nee)
Puzzle	*hoʻopohihihi* (ho-oh-poh-he-he-he)

Additional Vocabulary
A to Z—English/Hawaiian Common Words

Able (can)   *hiki* (he-key)

Abuse   *hana 'ino*
                          (hah-nah ee-no)

Ache   *'eha* (eh-hah)

Address (residence)   *wahi noho*
                          (vah-he no-ho)

Admire   *mahalo/makahehi*
                          (ma-hah-low)/(ma-kah-hey-he)

Adopt (foster child) *hānai* (hah-nye)

Adult   *makua* (ma-koo-ah)

Afraid   *maka'u* (ma-kah-oo)

Airplane   *mokulele*
                          (moh-koo-lay-lay)

Airport   *kahua ho'olulu mokulele*
                          (kah-who-ah ho-oh-lou-lou
                          moh-koo-lay-lay)

Ancient   *kahiko*
                          (kah-hee-koh)

Angry/Offended	*huhū* (who-who)
Apologize	*mihi* (me-he)
Ashamed	*hilahila* (he-lah-he-lah)
Ask	*nīnau* (nee-now)
Asleep	*hiamoe* (he-ah-moy)
Baggage/Luggage	*ukana* (oo-kah-nah)
Barbecue	*kō'ala* (koh-ah-lah)
Beard	*'umi'umi* (oo-me-oo-me)
Beautiful/Pretty	*u'i/nani* (oo-ee)/(nah-nee)
Begin	*ho'omaka* (ho-oh-ma-kah)
Beverage	*mea inu* (may-ah ee-noo)
Big/Large	*nui* (noo-ee)
Birth	*hānau* (hah-now)
Blind	*makapō* (ma-kah-poh)
Blood	*koko* (koh-koh)

Broil	*pūlehu*	
	(poo-lay-who)	
Brother	*kaikua'ana*	
	(ky-koo-ah-ah-nah)	
Busy	*pa'ahana*	
	(pah-ah-hah-nah)	
Busybody	*nīele* (nee-eh-lay)	
Can (tin)	*kini* (key-nee)	
Candy	*kanakē*	
	(kah-nah-kay)	
Canoe	*wa'a* (vah-ah)	
Canoe paddler	*hoe wa'a*	
	(hoy vah-ah)	
Care (to care for)	*mālama*	
	(ma-lah-ma)	
Careless	*kāpulu*	
	(kah-poo-lou)	
Carry (lift, transport)	*lawe* (lah-vay)	
Carry (pregnant)	*hāpai*	
	(hah-pie)	
Caucasian	*haole*	
(white person,	(how-lay)	
any foreigner)		

Celebrate	*ho'olaule'a* (ho-oh-lau-lay-ah)
Chant	*oli* (oh-lee)
Church	*hale pule* (hah-lay-poo-lay)
Closed	*pa'a* (pah-ah)
Club (organization)	*hui* (who-ee)
Continue	*ho'omau* (ho-oh-mow)
Cooked taro with water	*poi* (poy)
Correct	*pololei/pono* (poh-low-lay) /(poh-no)
Crazy	*pupule* (poo-poo-lay)
Crooked	*kapakahi* (kah-pah-kah-he)
Cry	*uē* (oo-way)
Curious (nosy person)	*nīele* (nee-eh-lay)
Damage	*pohō* (poh-ho)
Dead	*make* (ma-kay)
Deaf	*kuli* (koo-lee)
Dear (beloved)	*aloha* (ah-low-hah)

Delicious/Tasty	*'ono* (oh-no)
Desire	*makemake* (ma-kay-ma-kay)
Dirty	*lepo* (lay-poh)
Done (finished)	*pau* (pow)
Drink	*inu* (ee-noo)
Drum	*pahu* (pah-who)
Duty (obligation)	*pono* (poh-no)
Eat	*'ai* (eye)
Electric	*uila/uwila* (oo-we-lah)
Encore (to do it again)	*hana hou* (hah-nah ho)
Encourage	*ho'opaipai* (ho-oh-pie-pie)
Energetic (active/alert)	*'eleu* (eh-lay-oo)
Entertain	*ho'okipa* (ho-oh-key-pah)
Error	*hewa* (hey-vah)
Estate	*kuleana* (koo-lee-ah-nah)

Exercise (body)	*ho'oikaika kino* (ho-oh-ee-ky-kah key-no)
Fall	*hā'ule* (hah-oo-lay)
Famous	*kaulana* (cow-lah-nah)
Fast (quick)	*'āwīwī/wikiwiki* (ah-vee-vee)/(we-key-we-key)
Fat	*momona* (moh-moh-nah)
Favorite	*punahele* (poo-nah-hey-lay)
Fish	*i'a* (ee-ah)
Fish hook	*makau* (ma-cow)
Food	*'ai/mea 'ai* (eye)/(may-ah eye)
Forbidden (off limits)	*kapu* (kah-poo)
Force (strength)	*ikaika* (ee-ky-kah)
Friendship	*pilialoha* (pee-lee-ah-low-hah)
Full	*piha* (pee-hah)
Genealogy	*kū'auhau* (koo-ow-how)

Give	*hāʻawi* (hah-ah-vee)
God	*akua* (ah-koo-ah)
Gourd	*ipu* (ee-poo)
Grandparent	*kupuna* (koo-poo-nah)
Great/Large	*nui/nunui* (noo-ee)/(noo-noo-ee)
Ground/Earth/World	*honua* (ho-noo-ah)
Grumble (to complain)	*namunamu* (nah-moo-nah-moo)
Guardian	*kahu* (kah-who)
Handsome	*uʻi* (oo-ee)
Happy/Fun	*hauʻoli* (how-oh-lee)
Hawaiian feast (young taro tops)	*lūʻau* (lou-ow)
Heal	*lapaʻau* (lah-pah-ow)
Healthy/Alive/Life	*ola* (oh-lah)
Heaven	*lani* (lah-nee)
Help	*kōkua* (koh-koo-ah)

Hole/Opening	*puka* (poo-kah)
Hotel	*hōkele* (ho-kay-lay)
Hush	*hāmau* (hah-mow)
Idea	*mana'o* (mah-nah-oh)
Ignorant	*na'aupō/hūpō* (nah-ow-poh/who-poh)
Illness	*ma'i* (mah-ee)
Imitate	*ho'opili* (ho-oh-pee-lee)
Intelligent/Smart	*akamai* (ah-kah-my)
Jealous	*lili* (lee-lee)
Jug	*'ōmole* (oh-moh-lay)
Just (fair)	*pono* (poh-no)
Kick	*peku* (pay-koo)
Kiss	*honi* (ho-nee)
Knowledge	*ike/na'auao* (ee-kay/nah-ow-ow)
Labor	*hana* (hah-nah)

Land	*'āina* (eye-nah)
Language	*'ōlelo* (oh-lay-low)
Lazy	*moloā* (moh-low-ah)
Leader	*alaka'i* (ah-lah-kah-ee)
Legend	*mo'olelo* (moh-oh-lay-low)
Lei (necklace of flowers, shells, feathers, or all sorts of things)	*lei* (lay)
Lesson	*ha'awina* (hah-ah-vee-nah)
Line (cordage)	*kaula* (cow-lah)
Little	*li'i/li'ili'i* (lee-ee)/(lee-ee-lee-ee)
Lizard	*mo'o* (moh-oh)
Locals/Islanders	*kama'āina* (kah-ma-eye-nah)
Long (length)	*lō'ihi* (low-ee-he)
Look	*nānā* (nah-nah)

Loose/Unfastened	*hemo* (hey-moh)
Mail (letters)	*leka* (lay-kah)
Man/Husband	*kāne* (kah-nay)
Marijuana	*paka lōlō* (pah-kah low-low)
Market	*mākeke* (ma-kay-kay)
Mind (intellect)	*manaʻo* (ma-nah-oh)
Mosquito	*makika* (ma-key-kah)
Music	*mele* (may-lay)
Name	inoa (ee-no-ah)
Native	*kamaʻāina* (kah-ma-eye-nah)
Naughty	*kolohe* (koh-low-hay)
Navel	*piko* (pee-koh)
Newcomer	*malihini* (ma-lee-he-nee)
Noise/Noisy (Be quiet!)	*kulikuli* (koo-lee-koo-lee)
None/Nothing	*ʻaʻohe* (ah-oh-hay)

Occupation	*'oihana/hana* (oy-hah-nah / hah-nah)
Offend	*ho'ohuhū* (ho-oh-who-whoo)
Opinion	*mana'o* (ma-nah-oh)
Oven (underground)	*imu* (ee-moo)
Overcome (to defeat)	*lanakila* (lah-nah-key-lah)
Parent	*makua* (ma-koo-ah)
Party (large festivity)	*ho'olaule'a* (ho-oh-laow-lay-ah)
Party	*pā'ina* (pah-ee-nah)
Pay (payment)	*uku* (oo-koo)
Peace	*malu/maluhia* (ma-lou-he-ah)
Person	*kanaka* (kah-nah-kah)
Pet	*punahele* (poo-nah-hey-lay)
Picture	*ki'i* (key-ee)

Place of learning	*hālau* (hah-lau-oo)	
Poi pounder	*pōhaku ku'i 'ai* (poh-hah-koo koo-ee eye)	
Power	*mana* (ma-nah)	
Prayer	*pule* (poo-lay)	
Precious	*makamae* (ma-kah-my)	
Present (gift)	*makana* (ma-kah-nah)	
Priest	*kahuna* (kah-who-nah)	
Problem	*pilikia* (pee-lee-key-ah)	
Promise	*'ōlelo pa'a* (oh-lay-low pah-ah)	
Proud	*ha'aheo* (hah-ah-hay-oh)	
Pull	*huki* (who-key)	
Quick/Fast/Speedy	*'āwīwī/wikiwiki* (ah-vee-vee/we-key-we-key)	
Quiet	*mālie/ho'omālie* (ma-lee-eh/ho-oh-ma-lee-eh)	
Race (people)	*lāhui* (lah-who-ee)	
Race (contest)	*heihei* (hey-hey)	

Rainbow	*ānuenue* (ah-noo-eh-noo-eh)
Rascal	*kolohe* (koh-low-hay)
Ready/Prepared	*mākaukau* (ma-cow-cow)
Relative	*'ohana* (oh-hah-nah)
Repeat	*'ōlelo hou/hana hou* (oh-lay-low ho)/(hah-nah-ho)
Responsibility	*kuleana* (koo-lee-ah-nah)
Rice	*laiki* (lye-key)
Ride	*holo/holoholo* (ho-low-ho-low)
Righteous	*pono* (poh-no)
Rob	*'aihue* (eye-who-ee)
Rock (stone)	*pōhaku* (poh-hah-koo)
Rotten	*pilau* (pee-la-ow)
Rubbish	*'ōpala* (oh-pah-lah)
Sacred (off-limits)	*kapu* (kah-poo)
Sad	*kaumaha* (cow-ma-hah)
Salt	*pa'akai* (pah-ah-ky)
Sick	*ma'i* (ma-ee)

Sloppy/Poorly done	*kāpulu* (kah-poo-lou)
Smashed/Pulverized	*palahē* (pah-lah-hay)
Stick your nose where it doesn't belong	*maha'oi* (ma-hah-oy)
Stink (unpleasant odor)	*hauna* (how-nah)
Stomach/Abdomen	*'ōpū* (oh-poo)
Stupid	*lōlō* (low-low)
Taro	*kalo* (kah-low)
Teacher	*kumu* (koo-moo)
Tired	*māluhiluhi* (ma-lou-he-lou-he)
Tourist/Visitor	*malihini* (mah-lee-he-nee)
Trouble of any sort	*pilikia* (pee-lee-key-ah)
Turn/Turn over	*huli* (who-lee)
Ugly	*pupuka* (poo-poo-kah)
Upside down	*hulihia* (who-lee-he-ah)

Urgent	*koʻikoʻi* (koh-ee-koh-ee)
Urine	*mimi* (me-me)
Used to (accustomed)	*maʻa* (ma-ah)
Valley	*awaawa* (ah-vaah-vah)
Volcano	*lua pele* (lou-ah pay-lay)
Water	*wai* (vye)
Whoops! (Oh shucks!)	*auē/auwē* (ah-way)
Woman/Wife	*wahine* (wah-he-nay)/(vah-he-nay)
You	*ʻoe* (oy)
Young	*ʻōpio* (oh-pee-oh)
Zero	*ʻole* (oh-lay)

The Hawaiian Islands

O'ahu	(oh-ah-who)	Gathering Place
Hawai'i	(hah-vy-ee)	Big Island
Maui	(mow-we)	Valley Island
Kaua'i	(cow-wah-ee)	Garden Island
Lāna'i	(lah-nah-ee)	Pineapple Island
Moloka'i	(moh-low-kah-ee)	Friendly Island
Ni'ihau	(nee-ee-how)	Forbidden Island
Kaho'olawe	(kah-ho-oh-lah-veh)	The Taking Away

State Motto

Ua mau ke ea o ka 'āina i ka pono.
(oo-ah mow kay eh-ah oh kah eye-nah ee kah poh-no).

The life of the land is perpetuated in righteousness.

Also interpreted: Through righteousness the
sovereignty of the land has been restored.